Leaders

of the

Bible

Dr. Mapanza H Nkwilimba

Copyright © 2025 by Dr. Mapanza H Nkwilimba

All rights reserved. No part of this book may be reproduced or transmitted in any form or by any means without written permission from the author.

eBook ISBN: 978-9-69-709290-1

Paperback ISBN: 978-9-69-709291-8

Hardback ISBN: 978-9-69-709292-5

Dedication

For all the young dreamers and aspiring leaders, may the stories of courage, wisdom, and faith found within these pages inspire you to lead with integrity and compassion.

To the teachers and parents who nurture the next generation, instilling in them the values of kindness and resilience.

And to the leaders of today and tomorrow—may you carry the lessons of the past into a future filled with hope and purpose.

Table Of Contents

Foreword By Pastor Ronald Kalifungwa 1

Introduction 3

Chapter 1 Moses – The Courageous Leader 6

Chapter 2 David – The Heart of a True Leader 10

Chapter 3 Esther – The Brave Queen 16

Chapter 4 Nehemiah – The Builder of Dreams 21

Chapter 5 Jesus – The Ultimate Servant Leader 26

Chapter 6 Daniel – The Faithful Leader 31

Chapter 7 Paul – The Leader Who Shared the Message 36

Chapter 8 Your Leadership Journey Begins! 42

Foreword By
Pastor Ronald Kalifungwa

In a market flooded with leadership books, it's refreshing to find one specifically designed for children. Dr. Mapanza Nkwilimba's book, "Leaders of the Bible: Inspiring Leadership Adventures for Children," fills this gap, making it a unique and exciting resource.

I'm thrilled to introduce you to this amazing book, packed with wisdom from the Bible and Dr. Nkwilimba's extensive leadership experience. As a seasoned international leader, teacher and mentor, Dr. Nkwilimba has empowered many individuals, including children, to discover their leadership potential.

Within these pages, you'll encounter incredible biblical leaders like Moses, Esther, David, Daniel, Jesus, and Paul. You'll learn valuable lessons about kindness, courage, integrity, service, cooperation, and more!

Dr. Nkwilimba's message is clear: leadership is not just about achieving greatness, but about doing what's right, serving others, and making a positive impact in the world to the glory of God.

So, don't let your age hold you back! Start building your leadership skills now and inspire others to do the same. Remember Dr. Nkwilimba's words: "Take a deep breath, stand tall, and step forward on your leadership journey."

The world needs leaders like you! Take this book as your guide and embark on an amazing adventure. Become the leader you were meant to be and change our country and the world for the better!

Introduction

Welcome to "Leaders of the Bible: Inspiring Leadership Adventures for Children!" In a world where every child has the power to make a difference, this book invites you on an exciting journey through the stories of some of the greatest leaders in history—the characters of the Bible. Within these pages, you will discover remarkable individuals who embodied courage, kindness, integrity, and teamwork. These traits not only defined their leadership but also continue to inspire us today.

From the bravery of Moses as he led his people to freedom, to the unwavering faith of Daniel in the lions' den, and the compassionate service of Jesus, each chapter showcases how these biblical figures faced challenges and grew into extraordinary leaders. You will learn how their experiences can guide and empower you in your own life, teaching valuable lessons about standing up for what is right and making choices that reflect your values.

This book is not just a collection of stories. It is filled with engaging activities, discussions, and reflections designed to help you cultivate your own leadership skills. After reading each chapter, you will have the opportunity to put these lessons into practice, whether it's by planning a community event, creating a kindness calendar, or writing a pledge to stand strong in your beliefs.

As you turn the pages, remember that leadership is not limited to adults or those in charge—it lives within every child. You have the ability to inspire those around you, make a positive impact in your community, and shine brightly as a beacon of hope. The examples set by these biblical characters demonstrate that anyone can become a leader through dedication, compassion, and a willingness to learn.

So, are you ready to embark on this adventure? Together, let's explore the lives of these incredible figures and discover how you can begin your own leadership journey today. Get ready to learn, grow, and inspire, because the world needs leaders like you!

Let's dive in!

Chapter 1
Moses – The Courageous Leader

The Call of Moses

Once upon a time, in the land of Egypt, the Israelites were suffering as slaves under the rule of Pharaoh. They were hardworking and kind people, but they were treated unfairly and harshly. The cry of the Israelites reached the heavens, and God heard their pleas for help.

In a distant land, a baby boy named Moses was born. His mother loved him dearly and wanted to protect him from the cruel king's order to harm all Hebrew baby boys. So, she placed him in a basket and set him afloat on the river. Little did she know that this small act of love would change the course of history.

As the basket drifted along the river, it caught the eye of Pharaoh's daughter, who was bathing nearby. She saw the beautiful baby and felt compassion for him. Pharaoh's daughter decided to adopt Moses and raise him as her own son in the royal palace. Moses grew up in the lap of luxury but never forgot his true heritage as an Israelite.

One day, when Moses was a young man, he saw an Egyptian beating one of his fellow Israelites. Anger surged through him as he witnessed this injustice. In a moment of rashness, he intervened. To protect his people, he struck down the Egyptian, but this act led him to flee into the desert, feeling ashamed and afraid.

In the desert of Midian, Moses began a new life as a shepherd. For years, he cared for the sheep and spent time reflecting on his past and where he belonged. But God had a special plan for Moses that he could not yet see.

One day, while tending to his flock, Moses noticed a strange sight—a bush that was on fire but did not burn up. Curious, he approached the bush to take a closer look. Suddenly, a voice called out from the bush, "Moses! Moses!" Startled, Moses responded, "Here I am!"

"It is I, the God of your ancestors. I have heard the cries of my people, the Israelites. They are suffering in Egypt, and I have come to rescue them," said the voice from the bush. God continued, "I am sending you back to Egypt to lead my people out of bondage."

Moses was taken aback. "Me? How can I be the one to do this?" he questioned, feeling unworthy and afraid. He doubted his ability to confront Pharaoh and lead a whole nation. But God reassured him, saying, "I will be with you. Tell the people that I AM has sent you."

As Moses listened, he began to understand that his past experiences had shaped him for this important role. God chose him not because of his perfection but because of his heart and courage. With God's guidance, Moses would find the strength he needed to face Pharaoh and lead the Israelites to freedom.

Moses' Courageous Choice

Even though Moses felt nervous and unsure, he accepted the call. He gathered his courage, knowing he had a mission that was bigger than himself. With his brother Aaron by his side, he returned to Egypt, ready to confront Pharaoh and set his people free.

Lesson for Young Leaders
Moses teaches us that courage is not about being fearless, but about taking action even when we feel scared. Leadership often requires stepping out of our comfort zones and standing up for what is right.

Activity: Reflect and Write

Think about a time when you had to be brave or stand up for someone else. Write about what happened and how you felt. Remember, just like Moses, you can be a leader and help others, even when it seems difficult!

Thus, the journey of Moses as a courageous leader began, setting the stage for incredible events that would change the lives of many. Little did he know, his story would inspire countless generations to come!

Leaders of the Bible

Chapter 2

David – The Heart of a True Leader

The Shepherd Boy Who Became a King

In a small village called Bethlehem, there lived a young boy named David. He was not a warrior or a ruler; he was a humble shepherd who spent his days taking care of his father's sheep. David would sing to the animals, play his harp, and protect them from wild animals. Little did anyone know that this brave young boy was destined for greatness.

One day, a great challenge befell the Israelites. The fierce Philistines were threatening their land. Their champion, a giant named Goliath, stood over nine feet tall! Goliath wore heavy armor and carried a massive sword. Every day, he taunted the Israelites, challenging them to send out a warrior to fight him. The Israelite army was terrified; no one dared to face the giant.

David, bringing food to his older brothers at the battlefield, heard Goliath's cries. Instead of trembling with fear like the other soldiers, David felt a surge of courage rise within him. "Who is this giant that defies the army of the living God?" he exclaimed. David believed that with God on his side, he could defeat Goliath.

When David volunteered to fight the giant, King Saul was hesitant. "You are just a boy, and he has been a warrior since his youth!" the king said. But David replied, "I have fought off lions and bears to protect my sheep, and God has delivered me from them. He will deliver me from this Philistine too!"

King Saul finally agreed and offered David his armor, but it was too heavy. Instead, David chose to face Goliath with just his slingshot and five smooth stones from the brook. As he approached the giant, Goliath mocked him, but David stood firm.

With a brave heart and unwavering faith, David declared, "You come at me with a sword and a spear, but I come to you in the name of the Lord!" He spun his slingshot and released a stone that struck Goliath right between the eyes. The giant fell to the ground, defeated.

The Israelites cheered as David's bravery and faith saved them from their enemy. From that day forward, David became a hero in the land, and God had great plans for him as he would eventually become the king of Israel.

Activity: Your Own "Goliath Challenge"

Now it's time to think about your own "Goliath Challenge." What is a big goal or challenge you want to face? It could be trying something new, learning a skill, or even helping a friend. Here's how to create your challenge:

1. Identify Your Goliath: Write down a challenge that feels big and a bit scary, just like Goliath was for David.

2. Set Your Goal: Break it down into smaller, achievable steps. What can you do today that brings you closer to that goal?

3. Find Your Stones: Identify the resources or support you will need to reach your goal. This could be friends, family, or even practicing on your own.

4. Share Your Challenge: Share your "Goliath Challenge" with someone you trust. They can help cheer you on as you work towards it!

Leading with Kindness

While David was known for his bravery, he was also a kind leader. One of his most cherished friendships was with a boy named Jonathan, who was the son of King Saul. Though Jonathan was a prince and David was a humble shepherd, their bond was strong.

Jonathan recognized David's courage and loyalty, even when his own father was threatened by David's rising popularity. Instead of feeling jealous, Jonathan chose to support David and protect him, showing incredible loyalty. Their friendship exemplified what it means to lead with kindness.

David and Jonathan frequently encouraged each other and shared laughter. When Jonathan learned that his father wanted to harm David, he bravely warned him and helped him escape, proving that true friendship means putting others before ourselves.

Respecting and Caring for Friends

David taught us that part of being a great leader is respecting and caring for our friends. Just like David and Jonathan, we can show kindness by:

- Listening when our friends have something to say.

- Standing by them through tough times.

- Celebrating their successes and encouraging them to reach their goals.

Conclusion: The Heart of a Leader

David's story reminds us that leadership is not just about bravery but also about kindness, loyalty, and respect for others. Like David, we can embrace our challenges with courage while being compassionate to our friends.

In this way, we can all grow to be heart-filled leaders who uplift those around us!

Leaders of the Bible

Chapter 3
Esther – The Brave Queen

In a kingdom far away called Persia, there lived a young woman named Esther. She was known for her beauty and Bottom of Formgrace, but little did anyone know that she possessed an extraordinary bravery hidden within her heart. Esther was an orphan raised by her wise cousin, Mordecai, who taught her about her heritage and the importance of her people, the Israelites.

One day, the king of Persia, King Xerxes, held a grand contest to find a new queen. Young women from all over the kingdom were invited to present themselves before the king. Esther was hesitant at first, but Mordecai encouraged her, reminding her that perhaps she had a greater purpose.

When Esther arrived at the palace, something magical happened. She won the king's heart and was crowned queen. But amidst the glamour and luxury, there was a dark shadow looming over her people. A wicked advisor named Haman plotted to destroy all the Jews in the kingdom, and Esther soon learned that her beloved people were in grave danger.

With her heart pounding in her chest, Esther realized that she had to act. "I may be putting my life on the line, but I must speak for my people," she whispered to herself. But approaching the king was no small feat; if he didn't extend his golden scepter to her, she could be sentenced to death for even daring to enter his presence uninvited.

Esther knew she couldn't rush into this situation without careful thought. She took a moment to listen to her inner voice, to Mordecai's wise counsel, and to God's guidance. It was time to plan her approach with wisdom.

She drafted a heartfelt invitation and asked the king to join her for a special banquet. When the time came, Esther elegantly hosted King Xerxes and Haman, serving them exquisite food and drink. With each passing moment, she gathered her courage until finally, she revealed the truth about Haman's wicked plot against her people.

"Oh, King Xerxes," she implored, "spare my life and the lives of my people! For we are sold to be destroyed, and I am a Jewish girl standing right here before you."

The king, enraged upon learning Haman's treachery, ordered that Haman be punished, thus saving Esther's people. Thanks to Esther's bravery and wisdom, the Jewish people were rescued, and Esther became a shining example of courage in the face of danger.

Activity: Writing a Letter of Admiration

Just like Esther bravely communicated her needs to the king, it's your turn! Here's how you can write your very own letter to someone you admire:

1. Choose Someone to Write To: It could be a family member, friend, teacher, or public figure you respect.

2. Start with a Warm Greeting: Begin your letter with "Dear [Name],"

3. Acknowledge Their Impact: Write a few sentences about why you admire them. What have they done that inspires you?

4. Share a Personal Connection: Mention how their actions have affected you directly and what you've learned from them.

5. Express Your Gratitude: Thank them for being the person they are!

6. Close with Kindness: End your letter with a warm closing, such as "Sincerely" or "With admiration," followed by your name.

Once you've finished writing, why not send it? Imagine how happy it would make them to know how much they inspire you!

The Power of Listening and Planning

To make wise decisions, just like Esther, it's important to listen carefully to what others have to say. Listening allows us to understand different perspectives, gather valuable information, and even reflect on our own thoughts. Planning helps us prepare our actions thoughtfully and ensure that we are taking the right steps toward our goals.

Esther listened to her cousin Mordecai and carefully planned how to approach the king. She understood that her words had great power and that she needed to use them wisely. By taking time to listen and think it through, Esther was able to act courageously and save her people.

Conclusion: Thoughtful Decision-Making

Esther's story teaches us just how important it is to make thoughtful decisions and truly listen to those around us. Being a leader means being brave enough to stand up for what is right, but it also means being wise in our actions.

So next time you face a challenge or need to help someone, remember Esther's brave heart. Be sure to listen, plan carefully, and choose your words with love and kindness. You too can be a leader who inspires others and makes a difference in the world!

CHAPTER 4
Nehemiah – The Builder of Dreams

Rebuilding the Walls of Jerusalem

In a time long ago, the city of Jerusalem lay in ruins. Its once-mighty walls were broken, leaving the people vulnerable to their enemies. The streets were filled with rubble and sadness, and their hearts were heavy with despair. Among the people was a man named Nehemiah, a dedicated cupbearer to the king of Persia. Each day, as he tasted the king's wine, he couldn't shake the sorrow he felt for his hometown.

One fateful day, Nehemiah received news from a traveler about the crumbled walls of Jerusalem and the struggles faced by his people. His heart shattered, and the vision of a broken city haunted him. With determination igniting a fire within him, Nehemiah prayed fervently to God, seeking guidance and courage. He knew something had to be done.

Boldly, Nehemiah approached King Artaxerxes. His hands trembled at the thought of asking the king for help, but he believed in the mission ahead. "May I be sent to rebuild the walls of Jerusalem?" he requested.

To Nehemiah's surprise, the king granted his wish, providing him with letters of support and the resources he needed for the journey.

Upon arriving in Jerusalem, Nehemiah surveyed the walls under the cover of darkness. The sight was more heart-wrenching than he had imagined—old stones lay scattered, and despair hung over the people like a heavy fog. But Nehemiah was not one to give in to sorrow. Gathering the people together, he shared the vision God had placed in his heart: "We can rebuild these walls! With determination and teamwork, we will restore our city!"

The people felt a spark of hope as Nehemiah spoke. United by purpose, they rolled up their sleeves and got to work! Nehemiah organized groups of builders from different families and clans, assigning them specific sections of the wall to repair. Teamwork transformed the broken scene into a lively construction site filled with laughter and camaraderie.

As they worked, they faced challenges such as threats from their enemies and the heavy burden of the task ahead. Yet, Nehemiah's unwavering determination inspired the people to keep going. He encouraged them by saying, "Remember the Lord, who is great and awesome, and fight for your families!" This rallying cry fueled their spirits, and they remained committed even when the going got tough.

Day by day, stone by stone, the wall slowly took shape. The sound of hammers echoed, and soon, what once was a pile of rubble became a sturdy wall that surrounded Jerusalem once more. After just fifty-two days, the people of Jerusalem stood in awe at their achievement, realizing they had done the impossible through teamwork and belief in a shared vision.

Activity: Organizing a Community Project

Now it's your turn to experience the power of teamwork, just like Nehemiah! How about organizing a small community project with your friends or family? Here's how to get started:

1. Choose a Project: Think about a way you could help your community. Ideas could include cleaning up a local park, planting flowers in a community garden, or organizing a fun event for the neighborhood.

2. Gather Your Team: Invite friends, family, or classmates to help you with the project. Share the vision of what you want to achieve together!

3. Plan the Details: Discuss what needs to be done. Make a list of supplies you might need, such as trash bags, gloves, or gardening tools.

4. Set a Date: Pick a day when everyone can come together and make sure to let others in the community know about your project.

5. Celebrate Your Success: After your project, take time to celebrate what you accomplished together! Share pictures and stories about the experience.

Vision and Purpose: Leading Toward a Common Goal

Nehemiah's adventure shows us how having a clear vision helps leaders guide their teams toward a common goal. A vision is like a bright light that illuminates the path ahead, inspiring everyone along the way.

When Nehemiah gathered the people, he reminded them of the beauty of their home and how restoring the walls would bring safety to their families. This vision united everyone; suddenly, the difficult work became meaningful because they understood the purpose behind it.

As you think about your own community project, consider what vision you want to share with your team. A strong vision can motivate others and inspire them to work hard, just as it did for Nehemiah's builders.

Conclusion: The Power of Determination and Teamwork

Nehemiah's story teaches us the importance of determination, teamwork, and having a clear vision. When we work together toward a common goal, we can overcome even the greatest challenges. Remember, no task is too big when you have the faith, vision, and the help of your friends by your side!

Leaders of the Bible

Chapter 5
Jesus – The Ultimate Servant Leader

Teaching Through Service

In every corner of the world where stories of courage and kindness are told, there shines a name that brings hope and love: Jesus. He was more than just a teacher; He was the ultimate servant leader who changed hearts and lives forever.

From the moment Jesus began His ministry, He demonstrated what it truly meant to lead through service. Unlike many worldly leaders who sought power and riches, Jesus chose to lift others up by serving them, showing that greatness is found not in being served but in serving others.

Imagine the scene: Jesus walked among the people, teaching profound lessons with His words and actions. He healed the sick, comforted the broken-hearted, and fed the hungry. One of the most beautiful moments was when He washed the feet of His disciples. This act was usually reserved for servants, yet Jesus, the Son of God, took on this humble role to show that no task is too lowly for those who wish to lead with love.

When Jesus fed the 5,000 with just five loaves of bread and two fish, He didn't simply provide food; He shared love and compassion, reminding everyone that they were cared for. By teaching through service, Jesus inspired those around Him to do the same, encouraging them to live lives of gratitude and generosity.

Activity: Create a Kindness Calendar

Now it's time for you to be a servant leader like Jesus! Let's create a "Kindness Calendar" filled with acts of service that you can do throughout the week. Here's how to make one:

1. Gather Supplies: You'll need a piece of paper, colorful markers or crayons, and a ruler (if you want to make neat boxes).

2. Draw Your Calendar: Create a grid with seven boxes (one for each day of the week). You can decorate it with drawings of hearts, stars, or anything that represents kindness to you.

3. Plan Acts of Kindness: Each day, write down one act of kindness you can do. Here are some ideas to get you started:

    - Help a sibling with their homework.

    - Buy or make a treat for a neighbor.

- Write a thank-you note to someone who helps you.
- Volunteer to clean up a local park.
- Share a toy with a friend or donate clothes you no longer wear.
- Call or video chat with a family member you haven't seen in a while.
- Smile at someone and tell them they matter.

4. Track Your Kindness: As you complete each act, check it off or color it in! At the end of the week, celebrate the kindness you shared!

Leading with Compassion

Jesus was not only an incredible teacher but also the perfect example of leading with compassion. He understood the struggles of those around Him because He truly cared about their pain.

In the Gospel, we read about Jesus healing a blind man named Bartimaeus. Bartimaeus called out for help, and even when others tried to silence him, Jesus stopped and listened. With compassion, He healed Bartimaeus, restoring his sight. This beautiful story reminds us of the power of empathy—taking a moment to understand another person's struggles and showing them love through action.

Another touching moment was when Jesus met the Samaritan woman at the well. Society looked down on her, but He engaged her in meaningful conversation, offering her living water—symbolizing hope and renewal. This simple act of kindness transformed her life, reminding us that everyone deserves respect and compassion, regardless of their past.

Conclusion: The Heart of a Servant Leader

Through His life and deeds, Jesus teaches us that true leadership is rooted in serving others with love and compassion. By following His example, we can create a world filled with kindness, understanding, and generosity.

As you embark on your own journey of service and compassion, remember that every little act of kindness can make a big difference. You have the power to lead with love, just as Jesus did, and in doing so, you'll inspire others to join you on this beautiful path of servant leadership.

Leaders of the Bible

Chapter 6
Daniel – The Faithful Leader

The Courage of Daniel in the Lions' Den

In a magnificent kingdom ruled by King Darius, there lived a young man named Daniel. He was wise, intelligent, and dedicated to serving his king. Daniel's exceptional abilities caught the attention of the king, who favored him among his advisors. However, there was something even more remarkable about Daniel: his unwavering faith in God.

Daniel, a man of integrity, prayed to God three times a day, thanking Him and seeking guidance. This devotion, however, did not sit well with some jealous advisors who sought to remove him from power. They devised a clever plot to trap Daniel. They approached King Darius, persuading him to declare a decree that no one could pray to any god or human but the king himself for thirty days. Unaware of their malicious intentions, the king agreed, excited to strengthen his authority.

When the decree was announced, Daniel could have chosen to hide or remain silent. But instead, he remained steadfast in his beliefs. He continued to pray to God as he always had, unafraid of the repercussions. He was determined not to let fear silence his faith.

The jealous advisors swiftly caught Daniel in the act of prayer. They rushed to the king to inform him, reminding him that anyone who disobeys the decree must be thrown into the den of lions. King Darius was deeply troubled; he valued Daniel and was distressed to learn what had happened. Yet, he could not go back on his own command.

With heavy hearts, Daniel was led to the lions' den. As he stood in the darkness, he must have felt frightened, knowing the fierce lions awaited him. But in his heart, Daniel trusted God completely. He knew that God was with him, and he had faith that God would protect him.

The stone was rolled over the den, sealing Daniel's fate. That night, King Darius could not sleep, worried for his faithful friend. At dawn, he rushed to the den and called out to Daniel, "Has your God saved you?" To his astonishment, Daniel replied, "O king, live forever! My God sent His angel and shut the lions' mouths; they have not harmed me because I was found innocent in His sight!"

Through his unwavering faith and courage, Daniel emerged unharmed from the lions' den. The king, filled with joy and relief, ordered that Daniel be lifted out and declared the greatness of Daniel's God across the kingdom.

Activity: Write Your Own Pledge

Just as Daniel remained faithful to his beliefs, you can make a pledge to stand strong in your own values. Here's how to write your pledge:

1. Find a Quiet Space: Sit down with a notebook or a piece of paper.

2. Reflect on Your Beliefs: Think about what matters most to you. What do you believe in? Are there values that guide your actions, like honesty, kindness, and faith?

3. Write Your Pledge: Start with "I pledge to remain strong in my beliefs and values, just like Daniel." Follow this with specific promises you want to keep, such as:

    - "I will always tell the truth, even when it's hard."
    - "I will stand up for my friends when they need support."
    - "I will show kindness to others, regardless of the situation."

4. Sign and Date It: At the end of your pledge, write your name and the date. Keep it somewhere safe where you can read it often!

The Importance of Integrity

Daniel's story illustrates the importance of integrity, a quality that won him favor and respect among the leaders of his time. Integrity means doing what is right, even when no one is watching. It is standing firm in your beliefs and values no matter the challenges you face.

Despite the dangers he encountered, Daniel's integrity shone brightly. King Darius recognized Daniel's dedication and unwavering faith. His honesty and dedication not only protected him in the lions' den but also earned him a position of influence.

Because of Daniel's steadfastness, the king learned the powerful message of faithfulness and reverence for God. He even decreed that all people in the kingdom should honor Daniel's God. Daniel's integrity inspired everyone around him and left a lasting impact on the entire kingdom.

Conclusion: The Strength of Faith and Integrity

Daniel teaches us that true leadership is rooted in faith and integrity. By standing strong in our beliefs and acting with integrity, we can navigate life's challenges with courage, just like he did in the lions' den.

As you face your own challenges, remember Daniel's example—a faithful leader who relied on his faith and displayed unwavering integrity. You too can be a beacon of hope and strength, shining brightly for others to follow!

Leaders of the Bible

Chapter 7
Paul – The Leader Who Shared the Message

The Journey of Paul

In the early days of the Christian faith, there was a man named Paul who played a vital role in spreading the message of Jesus Christ far and wide. Originally known as Saul, he was once a strict opponent of Christianity, persecuting those who followed Jesus. However, one fateful day on the road to Damascus, Saul had a life-changing encounter with the risen Jesus Christ. Blinded by a brilliant light, he heard Jesus' voice calling out, transforming his heart and redirecting his life completely.

After this profound experience, Saul became Paul, a devoted follower of Christ. His passion for sharing the message of Jesus burned brightly, and he embarked on multiple journeys across different regions, including Asia Minor and Europe, traveling by land and sea. Paul preached in towns and cities, visiting synagogues and marketplaces, telling everyone about God's love and the good news of salvation.

During his travels, Paul faced many challenges. He was beaten, imprisoned, and faced hostility from those who opposed his message. Yet, through it all, Paul demonstrated remarkable resilience. Whenever he encountered hardship, he remained steadfast in his mission, remembering the purpose that drove him: to share the hope found in Jesus Christ. His faith was unshakable, inspiring others to persevere even in tough times.

Paul's letters to the communities he visited became powerful tools of encouragement. They were filled with wisdom and guidance, reminding believers of the importance of faith, love, and unity. His dedication to spreading the message of Jesus Christ helped establish early Christian communities and continues to inspire people today.

Activity: Planning a "Message Sharing" Event

Now it's time for you to take part in sharing a message of good news! Organizing a "Message Sharing" event with your friends or family can be a fun and meaningful way to connect. Here's how to set it up:

1. Invite Your Friends or Family: Gather a group of people who are eager to share uplifting messages.

2. Select a Date and Place: Choose a day and environment that works for everyone—this could be at home, in a park, or at school.

3. Create a Welcoming Space: Set up a comfortable area where everyone can sit together. You can add decorations or play soft music to create a positive atmosphere.

4. Encourage Participation: Ask each person to think of something they would like to share. They can consider:

    - A recent good deed they did or witnessed.
    - A lesson they learned that can inspire others.
    - A favorite story, quote, or Bible verse that brings them joy and hope.

5. Share and Listen: Allow each person to take turns sharing their messages. Everyone should listen attentively, and after each presentation, encourage them with cheers or applause!

6. Reflect Together: After everyone shares, discuss how these messages can impact your lives and the lives of others. How can you continue to spread good news beyond this event?

Teamwork in Mission

Paul's journeys illustrate the vital importance of teamwork in leadership. Throughout his travels, Paul didn't go alone; he traveled with companions like Barnabas, Silas, and Timothy. These partnerships were crucial not only for sharing the message but also for encouraging one another through challenges.

For example, during their first missionary journey, Paul and Barnabas worked side by side. They encouraged each other's strengths and supported each other in times of difficulty. When they faced rejection or danger, their collaboration helped remind them of their purpose: to bring hope and salvation to those who needed it.

Teamwork in leadership means recognizing that we are stronger together. Each person brings unique skills and perspectives, allowing a group to achieve more than one person could alone. Paul and his companions show us that by uniting our efforts, we create a powerful force for good.

Through teamwork, they celebrated successes together, strategized their missions, and prayed for one another. Each partner played an important role, inspiring trust, unity, and resilience. Whether they were praying together in prison or encouraging each other after facing adversity, their bond made each step of the journey possible.

Conclusion: Spreading Hope Together

The life of Paul teaches us that sharing the message of love and hope is both a courageous and essential journey. Through his travels, we learn the value of resilience even when faced with challenges. And by organizing your own "Message Sharing" event, you can spread joy and inspiration, just like Paul did.

Remember that teamwork is at the heart of leadership. Working alongside others allows us to lift each other up and shine brighter together. So embrace the power of collaboration, share your message with others, and become leaders of hope in your community!

CHAPTER 8
Your Leadership Journey Begins!

Congratulations, young leaders! You have embarked on an incredible journey through the pages of this book, discovering the remarkable stories of biblical characters who exemplified leadership in their lives. From Moses to Jesus to Paul, each of these figures has taught us valuable lessons about courage, integrity, service, and teamwork. Now, it's your turn to carry these lessons into the world!

Every child has the potential to be a leader—just like the characters we've explored together. Leadership is not only about holding a title or being in charge; it's about inspiring others, making kind choices, and standing up for what is right. It's about being a light in the world and using your unique gifts to help those around you.

As you go about your daily life, remember to embody the leadership traits you have learned:

- Be Courageous: Like David facing Goliath, do not be afraid to take risks and stand up for your beliefs.

- Practice Integrity: Follow Daniel's example by being honest and doing what is right, even when it is difficult.

- Serve Others: Follow the path of Jesus the Christ by showing love and compassion through acts of service, whether big or small.

- Work Together: Embrace teamwork as demonstrated by Paul and his companions, recognizing that by supporting one another, you can accomplish amazing things.

Every day is an opportunity to practice these skills. Whether you are in the classroom, at home, or in your community, you have the power to make a difference. Lead with kindness, encourage your friends, and always seek to uplift those around you.

As you reflect on the lessons from the Bible, remember that these characters are more than stories; they are relatable role models. They faced challenges, made mistakes, and learned along the way—just like you. By integrating these engaging stories and activities into your life, you are cultivating essential leadership skills inspired by timeless values.

The journey of becoming a great leader starts right now! With each act of kindness, courageous choice, and thoughtful decision, you are building a legacy of leadership that can inspire others. Remember, you are capable of amazing things, and by following the example of these biblical figures, you can lead the way to a brighter world.

Leaders of the Bible

So, take a deep breath, stand tall, and step forward on your leadership journey. As you go, carry with you the lessons learned from Moses, David, Esther, Jesus Christ, Daniel, and Paul. Your time to shine is here, and the impact you can make is limitless!

www.ingramcontent.com/pod-product-compliance
Lightning Source LLC
LaVergne TN
LVHW070939070526
838199LV00035B/655